A Crabtree Branches Book

TOP HIGH SCHOOL SPORTS

TRACK AND FIELD

Thomas Kingsley Troupe

Crabtree Publishing
crabtreebooks.com

School-to-Home Support for Caregivers and Teachers

This high-interest book is designed to motivate striving students with engaging topics while building fluency, vocabulary, and an interest in reading. Here are a few questions and activities to help the reader build upon his or her comprehension skills.

Before Reading:

- *What do I think this book is about?*
- *What do I know about this topic?*
- *What do I want to learn about this topic?*
- *Why am I reading this book?*

During Reading:

- *I wonder why...*
- *I'm curious to know...*
- *How is this like something I already know?*
- *What have I learned so far?*

After Reading:

- *What was the author trying to teach me?*
- *What are some details?*
- *How did the photographs and captions help me understand more?*
- *Read the book again and look for the vocabulary words.*
- *What questions do I still have?*

Extension Activities:

- *What was your favorite part of the book? Write a paragraph on it.*
- *Draw a picture of your favorite thing you learned from the book.*

TABLE OF CONTENTS

ON YOUR MARK

Your feet press against the **starting blocks**. Your fingers touch the concrete and your competition looks at you. You look up, focused on the distance ahead. The starting tone sounds and you launch yourself from the starting position. You're off!

Lace up your best shoes and get ready to run. We're about to learn why track and field ranks among the TOP HIGH SCHOOL SPORTS.

Usain Bolt

FUN FACT

Usain Bolt was the first man to win three consecutive Olympic gold medals in the 100-meter race. Bolt won them in 2008, 2012, and 2016.

TRACK AND FIELD HISTORY

Track and field is one of the oldest sports in the world. One of the first recorded races was held at the very first Olympics in 776 BCE.

This event was a 100-meter race called the stadion. The first stadion was one of five athletic events. It was won by a man named Coroebus of Elis. Coroebus was a cook, a baker, and an athlete. His prize for winning the first Olympic race? An olive wreath!

An olive branch is a a symbol of peace, victory, and honor, as well as the Olympic spirit.

The first Olympics were held in the valley of Olympia. They were held to honor the Greek god Zeus. After the first Olympics, they were held every four years until 393 CE.

Olympia Greece, site of the ancient Olympic Games

TRACK AND FIELD SEASON

In high school, track and field season usually starts in March or April. The timing depends on the region and weather.

Some athletes choose to participate in pre-season training in January or February. Workouts and **conditioning** help athletes prepare for the upcoming season.

FUN FACT

Track and field is one of the most affordable sports to participate in. Track athletes need good shoes and clothing appropriate to their sport. Most other "gear" is supplied by the school.

HIGH SCHOOL TRACK AND FIELD TEAMS

Depending on their size, high schools often have two track and field teams. The varsity team is usually made up of seniors and juniors. The school's strongest , fastest, and most experienced athletes compete on the varsity team.

Varsity teams often invite freshmen and sophomores with talent and skill to join.

Track and field participation has hit record numbers in recent years. Since 1971, the National Federation of State High School Associations (NFHS) in the United States has produced a high school sports participation survey. The most recent survey shows track and field is the second most popular sport for both boys and girls with a record 625,333 boys and 506,015 girls participating.

TRACK EVENTS: RUNNING AND RELAY

Track events are for running athletes. There are shorter **sprint** races that run 100 and 200 meters in length. Longer running events include the 800 meter, 1600 meter, or mile races, and races from 1,500 meters to 5,000 meters.

In addition, there are relay races where a **baton** is passed to each of the four racers. The event is won when the final racer of the group crosses the finish line first.

FUN FACT

A relay race runner can be disqualified if the baton is dropped or the handoff is sloppy. Baton control is crucial in these team races!

TRACK EVENTS: HURDLES

Another running event that combines both running and jumping is **hurdles**. They are frames that are placed throughout the track. Most hurdle races feature ten of them.

As the runner races along the track, they must jump over each hurdle. If they don't clear the hurdle or knock it down, they are not penalized. Hitting the hurdle just slows them down.

FIELD EVENTS: JUMPING

The high jump requires athletes to jump over a horizontal bar. Each time the bar is cleared, it is raised. They get three chances to clear the bar.

The long jump requires competitors to run and jump as far as they can into a sandpit. If they cross the line, it is considered a fault. They get three chances and judges use the longest jump.

FUN FACT

The record holder for the longest long jump is Mike Powell from the United States. He jumped 29 feet, 4 inches (8.95 m) on August 30th, 1991 at the World Championships in Athletics in Tokyo, Japan.

FIELD EVENTS: TRIPLE JUMP AND POLE VAULT

The triple jump requires timing and jumping distance. After running down a straightaway, athletes must hop, skip, and jump into a sandpit.

Pole vaulting requires athletes to run with a long, flexible pole made of fiberglass or carbon fiber. At the end of the stretch, they use the pole to launch themselves over a high bar. They fall into a cushioned pad on the other side.

FIELD EVENTS: THROWING

In discus, athletes attempt to throw a heavy disc as far as they can. They launch it from an 8.2 feet (2.5 m) circle.

The **javelin** throw requires athletes to throw a 7.5 to 8-foot (2.30 to 2.40 m) spear after running down a straightaway.

Shot put involves pushing a heavy metal bar as far as possible. Boys use a 12 pound (5.44 kg) and girls use a 8.8 pound (4 kg) shot.

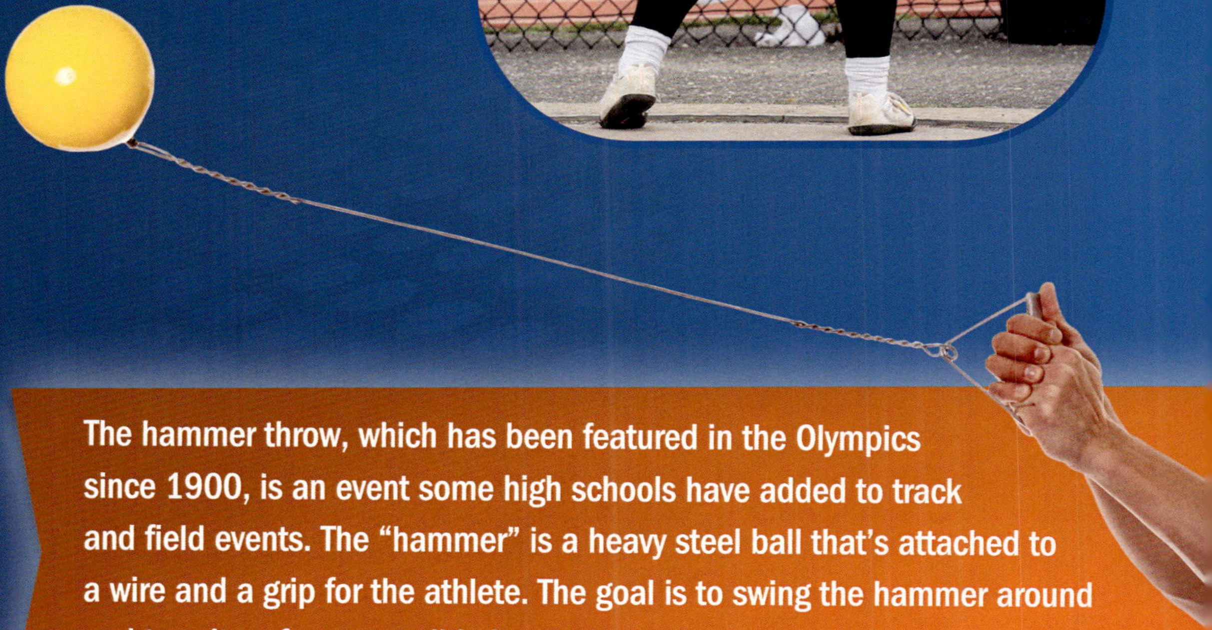

The hammer throw, which has been featured in the Olympics since 1900, is an event some high schools have added to track and field events. The "hammer" is a heavy steel ball that's attached to a wire and a grip for the athlete. The goal is to swing the hammer around and toss it as far as possible into a designated area.

PRACTICE AND TRAINING

Just as with any sport, it's important to train as much as possible. For running events, the best athletes run many times per week. Sprinters work on quick starts and distance runners focus on **endurance**.

Each field event is different, but practices can consist of **cardiovascular** exercise, strength, and flexibility training.

TRACK AND FIELD JARGON

There are a lot of strange terms, known as jargon, in track and field. Here are some of the most common.

Anchor — The last runner in a relay race team

Crossbar — The bar a high jumper or pole vaulter must clear

False Start — Moving or leaving starter blocks before the starting tone sounds

Impact Area — The designated spot where objects should land during throwing events

Runway — The stretch of straightaway an athlete runs before throwing or jumping

Toe the Line — To line up behind the white line before a race

ANCHOR

CROSSBAR

IMPACT AREA

PLAYOFFS AND STATE TOURNAMENTS

High school track and field teams compete with other schools to determine who's the best. Schools can participate in regional, state , provincial, or territorial meets as well as championship **tournaments**.

High school teams are broken into different **divisions** based on number or students, location, and skill level. This allows schools of all sizes to compete fairly!

FUN FACT

The heptathlon is an Olympic event for well-rounded track and field athletes! It combines seven events that are spread out over two days. They include the 100 meter hurdles, high jump, shot put, 200 meter race, long jump, javelin throw, and an 800 meter race!

CONCLUSION

Track and field is one of the most fast-paced and exciting high school sports. It takes, speed, endurance, strength, and skill to win. Fans love the variety of events at each meet.

Will you hit the track and race to victory? Will you jump or throw with the best of them? Maybe your team will win first place. With hard work and determination, you'll see why track and field is definitely one of the TOP HIGH SCHOOL SPORTS!

GLOSSARY

baton (buh-TON): A short stick or tube passed runner to runner in a relay race

cardiovascular (kahr-dee-oh-VAS-kyuh-ler): Relating to the heart and blood vessels

conditioning (kuhn-DI-shuh-nuhng): The process of training in order to become physically fit

consecutive (kuhn-SEK-yuh-tiv): Following one another in order, uninterrupted

divisions (dih-VIZH-uhnz): A grouping of teams or competitors according to skill, age, location

endurance (en-DUR-uhns): The ability or strength to continue or last, despite being exhausted

hurdles (HUR-dl): A race where athletes must leap over barriers places at spots around the track

javelin (JA-vuh-luhn): A light spear thrown in a competitive sport

sprint (SPRINT): To race or move at full speed, usually for a short distance

starting blocks (STAHR-ting bloks): Device used in track to help athletes brace their feet for a strong start

tournaments (TOOR-nuh-muhntz): A series of contests or games played between competing teams

INDEX

WEBSITES TO VISIT

https://kids.britannica.com/kids/article/track-and-field/353870

https://www.ducksters.com/sports/trackandfield.php

https://kids.kiddle.co/Track_and_field

ABOUT THE AUTHOR

Thomas Kingsley Troupe

Thomas Kingsley Troupe is the author of a big ol' pile of books for kids. He's written about everything from ghosts to Bigfoot to third grade werewolves. He even wrote a book about dirt. When he's not writing or reading, he gets plenty of exercise and remembers sacking quarterbacks while on his high school football team. Thomas lives in Woodbury, Minnesota with his two sons.

Written by: Thomas Kingsley Troupe
Designed by: Bobbie Houser
Series Development: James Earley
Editor: Ellen Rodger
Educational Consultant: Marie Lemke M.Ed.
Production manager: Candice Campbell
Prepress technician: Katherine Kantor

Photographs:
t = Top, c = Center, b = Bottom, l = Left, r = Right
Alamy: Lakeview Images: p. 6; Gary B: p. 7 b; H. Mark Weidman Photography: p. 11 t; Jeffrey Isaac Greenberg 18+: p. 13 t; Bob Daemmrich: p. 14; Enigma: p. 15 t; Paul Matzner: p. 19; Kirby Lee: p. 25 t; Bruce Leighty - Sports Images: p. 29 t
Dreamstime: Minacarson: cover t
Newscom: John Jones/Icon Sportswire DGA: cover b; Damon Higgins/ZUMA Press: p. 10; Ariel Fox/Image of Sport: p. 12; Dirk Shadd/ZUMA Press: p. 26; Allen Jr. Willie J./ZUMA Press: p. 27; Casey Christie/ZUMAPRESS: p. 28, p. 29 b
Shutterstock: WoodysPhotos: cover background, p. 1, p. 8 b, p. 9, p. 18, p. 21 t, p. 23 t, b; Stephen Mcsweeny: p. 4; Mark Herreid: p. 5 t, p. 17, p. 20 l; Petr TomanP: p. 5 b; vetre: p. 7 t; Bruce Yeung: p. 8 t; Aaron of L.A. Photography: p. 11 b; Apirakthanakorn: p. 13 b; cherrus: p. 15 b; JoeSAPhotos: p. 16; Brenda Carson: p. 20 r; Nicholas Piccillo: p. 21 b; LifetimeStock: p. 22; KOTOIMAGES: p. 24; Real Sports Photos: p. 25 bl; Esa Hiltula: p. 25 br

Crabtree Publishing

crabtreebooks.com 800-387-7650

Printed in the U.S.A./CP2025

Published in Canada
Crabtree Publishing
616 Welland Ave.
St. Catharines, Ontario
L2M 5V6

Published in the United States
Crabtree Publishing
347 Fifth Ave
Suite 1402-145
New York, NY 10016

Library and Archives Canada Cataloguing in Publication
Available at Library and Archives Canada

Library of Congress Cataloging-in-Publication Data
Available at the Library of Congress

Hardcover: 978-1-0398-8043-6
Paperback: 978-1-0398-8403-8
Ebook (pdf): 978-1-0398-8163-1
Epub: 978-1-0398-8283-6
Read-Along: 978-1-0398-8427-4
Audio book: 978-1-0398-8421-2